I LOVE
SHOW JUMPING

Coloring Book

Artist: Ellen Sallas

LRP

ISBN-13: 978-0692672143

Little Roni Publishers / Clanton, AL
www.littleronipublishers.com
@LittleRoniPublishers

Written and illustrated by
Ellen Sallas

PUBLISHED IN THE UNITED STATES OF
AMERICA

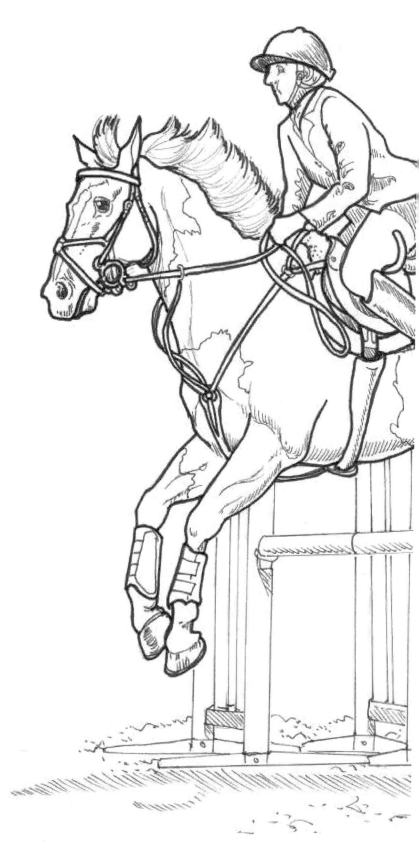

Many breeds of horses succeed in the sport of show jumping, but courage, scope, and athletic ability are necessary attributes to negotiate the obstacles presented at the upper levels.

Show jumpers are typically tall, over 16 hands, but smaller horses can be seen as well. Warmbloods are the first choice for many riders and trainers, although several breeds have found success up the levels.

Ponies compete in recognized show jumping competitions, often for youths under age 18, and are fun to watch as they negotiate the course. Most ponies have scrap and pluck, and always put on a good show.

Consistent quality training at home between competitions give the horse *and* rider strength, stamina, and confidence. The cross-rail with a pole ground line reinforces a straight approach and balanced effort needed for higher jumps.

Lungeing is used by riders and trainers of many disciplines. For show jumpers, a pre-class lunge session can work out bugs, as well as burn off excess nervous energy.

Show jumpers spend a portion of their training perfecting the movements of dressage, which increase suppleness, balance, and flexibility.

A huge effort coupled with an unprepared rider can result in an exciting landing on the other side. Staying in the saddle can prevent elimination.

Show jumping obstacles are generally negotiated from a forward canter or even controlled gallop. Falls can be dramatic, but rarely result in serious injury.

British show jumping evolved in 18th century England when new laws required fences be erected around properties. Suddenly, foxhunters needed to be able to leap these fences to hunt. Voila! "Horse leaping" grew into a sport from there.

Before Italian horse trainer, Captain Caprilli, developed the forward seat we use today, riders rode with long stirrups and leaned back over the fences.

Tied entries usually have a jump-off over a raised and shortened course, and the course is timed. If entries are tied for faults accumulated in the jump-off, the fastest time wins.

Canadian Olympian Ian Millar bought Belgian Warmblood, Big Ben, for $45,000. The giant 17.3 hand gelding won more than $1.5 million in his show career. Millar kept him for his entire life, and Big Ben's gravesite is located at Millar's farm.

Much loved by spectators and photographers, the famous *Derby Bank* at the British Jumping Derby has a 3'5" fence atop a 10'6" drop, which the horse must slide down.

Run under International Federation for Equestrian Sports (FEI) rules, Grand Prix is the highest level of show jumping. The horse jumps a course of 10-16 obstacles, with heights up to 1.6 meters (5 feet 3 inches) and spreads of up to 2.0 metres (6 ft 7 in).

An "oxer" is a type of fence with two verticals close together, sometimes called a "spread." A "square oxer" has both top poles at the same height.

Eventing (also called Horse Trials) is built of three phases, stadium jumping being one of those. The height and difficulty of the obstacle question is determined by the level entered, Beginner Novice through Advanced.

The *open water* obstacle is a large, rectangular-shaped "ditch" of water, often with a small brush or a rail on one side to act as a ground line. Water jumps are one of the widest obstacles a horse will be asked to jump, with a width up to 16 ft.

The open water obstacle should be approached strongly, and the rider must judge the take-off to put the horse as deep to the obstacle as possible. It is also important for the rider to keep his or her eyes up and not over-ride in exuberance.

Considered one of the premier events in the equestrian calendar, the British Jumping Derby is an annual showjumping event held in June since 1961 at the All England Jumping Course at Hickstead.

Jump judges are utilized on course and must pass a stringent application to be accepted. For FEI competitions, two of the many requirements are the applicant must speak French or English and be 50 years or older.

Show jumping obstacles are usually colorful and creative, and often paid for by sponsors whose name or logo appears on the fence.

Bridles and bits are subject to very few rules. Riders will use whatever works best for them. The ground jury will always have the last say if the equipment is too severe, but very rarely would this be an issue.

Nearly all jumpers will wear leg protection. Most common on the forelegs are open-front tendon boots. These protect the sensitive back of the leg, but allow the horse to feel if it rubs a fence.

After a clear and victorious round, this horse and rider enjoy a victory lap down the long side toward the exit.

Show jumping is one of many equestrian disciplines that truly fosters a sense of partnership between horse and rider.

(Sample art from "I Love Dressage Coloring Book" by Ellen Sallas)

Look for these coloring books by Ellen Sallas,
from Little Roni Publishers

- I LOVE RIDING LESSONS
- I LOVE CROSS-COUNTRY
- I LOVE DRESSAGE
- I LOVE TRAIL RIDING
- I LOVE PONIES
- I LOVE HUNTER/JUMPER
- I LOVE WESTERN RIDING
- COLOR ME SPLASHY
- EAT, SLEEP, HORSES
- BEEN THERE, DONE THAT (SPILLS)
- MY EQUINE VALENTINE
- SILLY HORSES
- EQUESTRIAN PARADE

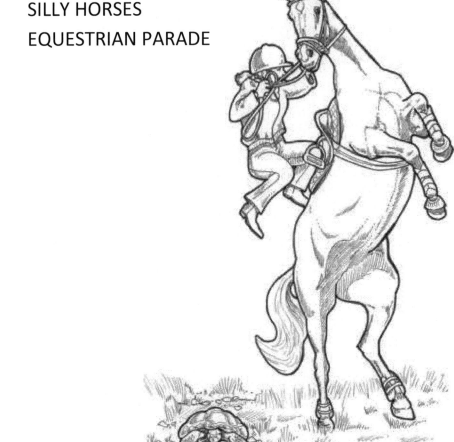

REAL HORSE ART THAT YOU COLOR, FRAME, AND HANG!

A SPECIAL COLORING BOOK FOR HORSE LOVERS

ABOUT THE ARTIST

Bestselling author and artist Ellen Sallas has been drawing horses even before she could walk. An avid horse lover herself, Ellen has been known to ride horses over hill and dale while daydreaming about stories yet written.

Ellen lives with her husband and vivid imagination in North Alabama.

Ellen has sold her art worldwide as an acclaimed animal portraitist for nearly thirty years. You can purchase prints and originals at https://www.etsy.com/shop/giddyupstudio or by email, ellenmaze@aol.com.

Ellen and Amber competing at J3 in Mississippi

Ellen and Amber at Foxwood Farms Eventing Barn in Pike Road, AL

www.ellencmaze.com

www.EquestrianColoringBooks.com

*Coloring page from Ellen Sallas's EAT SLEEP
HORSES An Adult Coloring Book for Equestrians*

www.LittleRoniPublishers.com

Made in the USA
Columbia, SC
01 December 2021

50002014R00020